Healthy Meat

Dee Laffan

WP

Published by:
Wilkinson Publishing Pty Ltd
ACN 006 042 173
Level 4, 2 Collins St Melbourne,
Victoria, Australia 3000
Ph: +61 3 9654 5446
www.wilkinsonpublishing.com.au

International distribution by Pineapple Media Limited
(wwwpineapple-media.com) ISSN 2203 0840

National Library of Australia Cataloguing-in-Publication data:

Author:	Laffan, Dee, author.
Title:	Healthy meat : lean recipes that don't compromise on taste / Dee Laffan.
ISBN:	9781922178763 (paperback)
Subjects:	Cooking (Meat) Low-fat diet—Recipes.
Dewey Number:	641.66
Layout Design:	Tango Media Pty Ltd
Cover Design:	Tango Media Pty Ltd
Editor:	Jess Lomas

Photos and illustrations by agreement with Easy Food Magazine.

Contents

Dee Laffan is editor of *Easy Food* magazine, Ireland's best-selling monthly food magazine, and has been part of the food media in Ireland for almost 10 years, previously working as a freelance editor and food columnist for many Irish magazines and newspapers. She is also a member of the Irish Food Writers' Guild. Dee is passionate about food and a proud supporter of Irish food and its producers. She loves cooking and trying out new ingredients and recipes at home for inspiration for the magazine.

Easy Food is Ireland's number one food magazine. It was created in 2003 and has been the best-selling monthly food publication in Ireland for the past 10 years. It is the ultimate cooking and kitchen companion for home cooks; a go-to guide for simple everyday recipes, handy cooking tips and miscellaneous kitchen know-how. It is aimed at budget-conscious, time poor, nutritionally aware home cooks that are looking for simple, yet tasty meal solutions for any occasion.

The magazine is distributed in 23 countries, with a digital version available through the newsstand app for android and Apple, and its website has a searchable recipe database with thousands of delicious recipes and step-by-step videos.

Visit: *www.easyfood.ie.*

Introduction

Did you read the title of this book and say to yourself, 'Is there such a thing as healthy meat?' The answer is yes. This is because of numerous factors including; how often you eat meat, choosing the right type of meat, the cut of meat, traceability of meat, and how it is cooked.

Meat, in particular red meat, can often be the target of accusations of high-cholesterol, high blood pressure and gut-related illnesses, to name but a few. There are even some studies that argue we should be eating less of it and adopting a vegetarian or vegan diet to sustain a healthier, longer life. While it is true that a diet rich in vegetables and fruit has countless benefits, there are also ways to enjoy meat without feeling unhealthy.

By choosing lean, cuts you'll be saving yourself extra fat and calories, and instead be filling up on all the great protein and nutrients that meat has to offer. The real problem lies in the developing tendancy to overeat and indulge in one segment of the food pyramid too much, for example, meat or carbs. Therefore the key to a healthy diet is finding the right balance, so that we can enjoy all of our favourite ingredients and foods, even the less healthy ones, in moderation.

It's best to eat less processed meat, such as sausages, bacon, ham, salami and pâtés, as they have a higher risk of causing diseases.

Meats such as chicken, pork, lamb and beef are all rich in protein. However, poultry has the lowest carbon footprint of any meat, and turkey is also a good choice. Opt for organic, free-range (pasture-raised) or antibiotic-free, if possible, but avoid less healthy processed forms for the lowest environmental impact.

When buying meat, go for the leanest option. As a rule, the more white marbling you can see in meat, the more fat it contains. So, for example, back bacon contains less fat than streaky bacon.

These tips can help you buy healthier options:

- Ask your butcher for a lean cut.
- If you're buying pre-packed meat, check the nutrition label to see how much fat it contains and compare products.
- Go for turkey and chicken without the skin, as these are lower in fat.
- Try to limit meat products in pastry, such as pies and sausage rolls, because they are often high in fat and salt.

When cooking meat, it is important not to add any unnecessary extra fat to the dish by cooking it in a lot of oil. Only use extra when needed and use healthy oils such as Rapeseed or coconut. There are also a few other tips you can do:

- Cut off any visible fat and skin before cooking – crackling and poultry skin are much higher in fat than the meat itself.
- Grill meat, rather than frying.
- Roast meat on a metal rack above a roasting tin so the fat can run off.
- Try using smaller quantities of meat and more vegetables, pulses and starchy foods.

Keeping all of this in mind when we were creating the content for *Healthy Meat*, we've packed each chapter with well-balanced, quick and easy, healthy recipes. We've also included a chapter called *Perfect Sides*, which includes delicious seasonal salads that are a perfect partner to any meaty main, and there are even some vegetarian dishes in our chapter *Mighty and meatless*, which are meals with so much bite you wouldn't even know they don't have meat in them.

Enjoy!

Budget-Friendly | Freezable | Kid-Friendly | LF Low-Fat | DF Diabetes-Friendly | GF Gluten-Free

Healthy ways with red meat

Asian beef and lettuce wraps

Serves 4

400g (14oz) beef mince
2 tsp vegetable oil
1 onion, chopped
2 garlic cloves, chopped
1 tbsp soy sauce
5 tbsp hoisin sauce
3cm (1.5 inch) piece of ginger, peeled and grated
1 tbsp rice wine vinegar
6 spring onions (scallions), chopped
2 tsp sesame oil

To serve:
16 butterhead (Boston) lettuce leaves

1. Heat the mince in a frying pan over a medium heat for 5-7 minutes until cooked through, stirring with a wooden spoon to break it into small pieces. Transfer to a plate and wipe out the pan with kitchen paper.

2. Heat the oil in the pan and cook the onion for five minutes until soft. Stir in the remaining ingredients and cook for two minutes until the spring onions begin to wilt. Stir the beef back into the pan and cook until it is heated through.

3. Divide the meat mixture among the lettuce leaves, wrapping the lettuce around the beef to eat.

Per serving: *295kcals, 11.5g fat (3.3g saturated), 13.8g carbohydrates, 7.2g sugars, 32.1g protein, 1.7g fibre, 0.61g sodium*

LF DF

Beef and black bean noodles

Serves 4

2 tbsp black bean sauce
1 tbsp hoisin sauce
60ml (1/4 cup) chicken stock
350g (12.5oz) thin noodles
1 tbsp peanut oil (or sunflower oil)
350g (12.5oz) lean minced beef
1/2 head broccoli, cut into small florets
4 spring onions (scallions), cut into 3cm (1.5 inch) lengths
100g (1 cup) bean sprouts
2 small cucumbers, halved lengthways, seeds removed, sliced
A handful of fresh coriander (cilantro) leaves

1. Combine black bean sauce, hoisin sauce and stock in a jug. Place the noodles in a heatproof bowl. Cover with warm water and leave to stand for three minutes. Drain and separate noodles.

2. Heat a wok over a high heat until hot. Add two teaspoons of oil and the mince. Cook, stirring, for 2-3 minutes or until browned. Transfer to a plate and cover to keep warm.

3. Add the remaining oil, broccoli and spring onion to the wok. Stir-fry for 3-4 minutes or until the broccoli is tender.

4. Add the noodles, sauce mixture and mince. Cook for two minutes or until heated through. Spoon into serving bowls and top with bean sprouts, cucumber and coriander.

Per serving: *410kcals, 11.7g fat (3.2g saturated), 41.6g carbohydrates, 9.8g sugars, 36.1g protein, 5.3g fibre, 0.44g sodium*

LF

Beef medallions and balsamic sauce

Serves 4-6

1 tbsp olive oil
1 tbsp shallots, finely chopped
1 garlic clove, minced
230ml (1 cup) balsamic vinegar
1½ tsp sugar
1 tsp rosemary, chopped
1 tsp Dijon mustard
Cooking spray
450g (16oz) beef medallions, cut into slices
Salt and black pepper

To serve:
Mixed salad

1. Heat the oil in a small saucepan over a medium heat. Add shallots and garlic and cook for two minutes.

2. Stir in the vinegar, sugar, rosemary and mustard and cook for five minutes, until reduced by half.

3. Lightly coat a large frying pan with cooking spray and heat over a medium-high heat. Season the beef with salt and pepper and cook for three minutes per side.

4. Add the balsamic reduction and cook for one minute, turning the beef to coat it in the sauce. Serve warm with a side salad.

Per serving: *22kcals, 6g fat (1.3g saturated), 13.6g carbohydrates, 1.2g sugars, 14.5g protein, 0.1g fibre, 400mg sodium*

LF DF

Easy burger salad

Serves 4

600g (21oz) beef mince
4 tbsp (¼ cup) ketchup
1 tbsp mustard
2 tbsp Worcestershire sauce
2 hamburger buns, cut into cubes
50g (3½ tbsp) butter, melted
2 heads of lettuce, shredded
120g (1 cup) Cheddar, grated
2 tomatoes, chopped
1 red (Spanish) onion, chopped

1. Heat the mince in a frying pan over a medium heat, using a wooden spoon to break it into chunks. Drain off the fat.

2. Stir in the ketchup, mustard and Worcestershire sauce until combined. Warm over a low heat for 20 minutes.

3. Preheat the oven to 180°C/160°C fan/gas mark 4/350°F. Toss the cubed hamburger buns with the butter on a baking tray. Bake for 10-15 minutes until browned.

4. Divide the lettuce among serving plates and top with the meat mixture, some Cheddar, tomatoes and onion.

5. Sprinkle the toasted croutons around the plate and serve warm or at room temperature.

Per serving: *604kcals, 25g fat (10.2g saturated), 32.9g carbohydrates, 13.2g sugars, 62.5g protein, 8.7g fibre, 0.78g sodium*

Horseradish steak and potatoes

Serves 4

450g (16oz) new potatoes
340g (12oz) green beans, trimmed
A small handful of fresh chives, chopped
2 corns on the cob
450g (16oz) sirloin steak, fat trimmed
Salt and black pepper
60ml (4 tbsp) low-fat sour cream
3 tbsp white wine vinegar
2 tbsp horseradish sauce
1 tbsp Worcestershire sauce
2 tbsp plus 1 tsp extra virgin olive oil

1. Steam the potatoes for 10-15 minutes until tender. Transfer to a cutting board to cool. Alternatively, boil the potatoes in a large saucepan of water.

2. Steam the beans for 4-6 minutes until bright green and just tender. Rinse with cold water until cool and transfer to a large bowl. If boiling the potatoes, add the beans during the last two minutes of cooking and drain.

3. Cut the potatoes into wedges and add to the bowl with the beans. Stir in the chives.

4. Heat a grill pan to a medium-high heat and grill the corn for 8-12 minutes, turning occasionally until charred and tender.

5. Season the steak with salt and pepper. Rub the steaks with one teaspoon of oil and cook for 3-4 minutes per side.

6. Meanwhile, stir together the sour cream, vinegar, horseradish, Worcestershire and a pinch of pepper in a small bowl. Whisk in the remaining oil until combined.

7. Transfer the steak and corn to a cutting board. When the corn is cool enough to handle, cut the kernels from the cob.

8. Allow the steak to rest for five minutes then thinly slice crosswise.

9. Add the steak – along with any accumulated juice – and the corn to the bowl with the potatoes and beans. Toss with the horseradish dressing and serve warm.

Per serving: *444kcals, 17.6g fat (5.1g saturated), 32.9g carbohydrates, 5g sugars, 39.4g protein, 6.8g fibre, 0.18g sodium*

DF

Low-fat summer steak

Serves 4

400g (14oz) sirloin steak, fat trimmed
Salt and black pepper
1 red (Spanish) onion, thickly sliced
3 tbsp lime juice
1 tbsp honey
2 tsp olive oil
1 tsp smoked paprika
½ tsp chilli flakes
½ cantaloupe melon, peeled, deseeded and cut into thin wedges
A handful of fresh coriander (cilantro), chopped
A handful of fresh mint, chopped

1. Heat a grill pan or barbecue over a medium-high heat and coat with cooking spray. Season the steak with salt and pepper and cook for three minutes per side for medium-rare. Remove from the heat and cover loosely with foil.

2. Add the onion and cook for eight minutes, flipping once.

3. Whisk together the lime juice, honey, oil, paprika and chilli flakes.

4. Slice the steak and arrange on a serving dish with the melon, coriander and mint. Drizzle over the dressing to serve.

Per serving: *250kcals, 8.7g fat (2.7g saturated), 11.2g carbohydrates, 8.6g sugars, 31.1g protein, 1.2g fibre, 0.07g sodium*

LF DF GF

Minty lamb chops

Serves 4

8 lamb chops
Salt and black pepper
1½ tbsp balsamic vinegar
½-1 tsp sugar, or to taste
4 tbsp (¼ cup) olive oil
A large handful of fresh mint leaves, chopped
2 garlic cloves, chopped

To serve:
Baby potatoes, boiled

1. Season the lamb chops with salt and pepper and set aside in a baking dish. Whisk together the vinegar, sugar and oil. Stir in the mint leaves and half of the garlic. Pour on top of the lamb and leave to marinate for at least 30 minutes.

2. Heat a grill pan to a medium-high heat. Shake off any excess marinade from the lamb chops and cook for 3-4 minutes per side.

3. Serve two lamb chops per person with the potatoes and remaining marinade drizzled over the top.

Per serving: *444kcals, fat 26.2g (6.3g saturated), 1.6g carbohydrates, 1g sugars, 47.8g protein, 0.13g sodium*

DF GF

Minute steak with asparagus

Serves 4

1 garlic clove, crushed
2 tbsp balsamic vinegar
2 tbsp olive oil
Salt and black pepper
1 bunch of baby asparagus, spears trimmed
8 thin (minute) steaks
A handful of fresh flat-leaf parsley, chopped
1 tbsp pine nuts, toasted

1. Whisk together the olive oil, garlic, vinegar, salt and pepper in a small bowl.

2. Place the asparagus on a large plate and drizzle with the oil mixture. Set aside for 10 minutes.

3. Heat a griddle pan over a high heat. Brush the steak with a little extra olive oil and season with salt and pepper. Cook the steak for 30 seconds on each side or until cooked to your liking. Transfer to a plate and cover with foil to keep warm.

4. Add the asparagus to the grill and cook, turning occasionally, for 3-4 minutes or until tender.

5. Serve the steaks with the asparagus.

Per serving: *551kcals, 22.2g fat (5g saturated), 2.6g carbohydrates, 0.9g sugars, 81.2g protein, 1g fibre, 0.1g sodium*

LF DF GF

Roasted red pepper lamb chops

Serves 4

8 lamb chops, excess fat trimmed
1 red (Spanish) onion, sliced
2 red peppers (capsicums), deseeded and sliced
1 tbsp olive oil
60g (2oz) mint sauce
Salt and black pepper
¼ tsp dried marjoram leaves

1. Preheat the oven to 220°C/200°C fan/gas mark 7/425°F and line a baking tray with foil. Arrange the lamb chops, onion and red pepper slices on the tray and toss with the oil. Bake for 10 minutes.

2. Stir together the remaining ingredients in a saucepan over a medium heat, then brush over the lamb chops and vegetables. Bake for another 10 minutes, brushing occasionally with the sauce, until the lamb chops are medium rare and the vegetables are tender.

Per serving: *382kcals, 16.5g fat (5.1g saturated), 5.8g carbohydrates, 2.3g sugars, 50.3g protein, 1.9g fibre, 0.2g sodium*

DF

Steak salad

Serves 4

750g (26.5oz) steak
4 tbsp (¼ cup) olive oil
2 tsp cumin seeds
4-5 courgettes (zucchinis), sliced into thin batons
2 red peppers (capsicums), deseeded and cut into strips
2 tbsp red wine vinegar
1 garlic clove, crushed
½ -1 red chilli, deseeded and finely chopped
20g (1 cup) rocket (arugula) leaves
Salt and black pepper

1. Preheat the grill to medium-high. Brush the steak on both sides with 1 tbsp of olive oil, and then rub both sides with pepper and cumin seeds.

2. Grill the steak for 3-4 minutes on each side for medium rare, or until cooked to your preference. Remove from under the grill, cover with tin foil and leave to stand for five minutes before slicing diagonally into strips.

3. Cover a baking tray with tin foil and place under the grill. In a large bowl, toss the courgettes and peppers with 2 tbsp of the remaining olive oil, then grill for 4-6 minutes or until tender. Remove from the heat.

4. To make the dressing, whisk the remaining tablespoon of olive oil with the vinegar, garlic and chilli in a bowl, season with salt and pepper.

5. Place the rocket leaves in a large serving bowl and top with the steak, courgette and peppers. Pour over the dressing and toss well to combine.

Per serving: *423kcals, 24.2g fat (5.6g saturated), 6.7g sugars, 45.5g protein, 1g fibre, 0.22g sodium*

LF DF GF

Lean not mean

BBQ lime chicken

Serves 4

2 garlic cloves, crushed
Juice and zest of 2 limes
5 tbsp (1/3 cup) olive oil
450g (16oz) chicken thighs
2 tomatoes, sliced
2 cucumbers, halved lengthways and sliced
1 red (Spanish) onion, thinly sliced
2 tbsp fresh coriander (cilantro), chopped
4 flour tortillas
Non-stick cooking spray
2 tsp chilli powder

To serve:
Lime wedges
Mixed salad leaves

1. Combine the garlic, two tablespoons of lime juice and 60ml (1/4 cup) of oil in a baking dish. Add the chicken, season with salt and pepper and turn to coat.

2. In a separate bowl, add the tomatoes, cucumber, onion and coriander. Drizzle with the remaining oil and one tablespoon of lime juice. Toss to combine.

3. Heat the barbecue to a medium-high heat. Add the chicken and cook for 5-6 minutes on each side or until cooked through.

4. Spray each side of the tortillas with the cooking spray and sprinkle with the chilli powder. Cook for 1-2 minutes on each side or until brown and crisp. Cut into wedges.

5. Sprinkle the chicken with the lime zest and serve with lime wedges, salad and tortilla wedges.

Per serving: *484kcals, 28.1g fat (5g saturated), 22.8g carbohydrates, 5.5g sugars, 36.1g protein, 4.2g fibre, 0.16g sodium*

LF DF

Grilled chicken and artichoke flatbread

Serves 4

2 chicken fillets
3 tbsp olive oil
Salt and black pepper
4 whole-wheat flatbreads
3 tbsp olive oil
115g (1 cup) goat's cheese, crumbled
120g (4 cups) spinach leaves
170g (1 cup) artichoke hearts, drained and chopped
1 tomato, chopped

1. Heat a barbecue or a grill pan to a medium heat. Rub the chicken with a bit of oil and season with salt and pepper. Grill for 10-12 minutes, flipping once, until cooked through. Allow to rest then shred into pieces when cool enough to handle.

2. Brush a bit of the oil on both sides of the bread. Cook on one side for two minutes until lightly charred.

3. Spread the grilled side of the flatbread with the goat's cheese, then top with the spinach, artichokes, tomato and chicken. Season with salt and pepper.

4. Return to the grill and cook for three more minutes, until the toppings are heated through. Serve warm.

Per serving: *452kcals, 32.2g fat (8.4g saturated, 16.1g carbohydrates, 11.6g sugars, 26.4g protein, 6.2g fibre, 0.59g sodium*

Honey soy chicken kebabs

Serves 6

1 tbsp vegetable oil
2 tbsp honey
2 tbsp soy sauce
¼ tsp black pepper
8 boneless, skinless chicken fillets, cubed
2 garlic cloves, crushed
5 onions, cut into wedges
2 red peppers (capsicums), cut into squares
12 skewers

To serve:
Brown rice, cooked according to packet instructions

1. Whisk together the oil, honey, soy sauce and pepper. Set aside a small amount to brush onto the kebabs as they cook.

2. Add the chicken, garlic, onions and peppers to the bowl and marinate in the refrigerator for at least 30 minutes (the longer the better).

3. Heat a grill pan over high heat.

4. Drain marinade from the chicken and vegetables and discard. Thread the chicken and vegetables alternately onto the skewers.

5. Lightly oil the grill pan. Cook kebabs for 12-15 minutes, until chicken is cooked through. Turn and brush with reserved marinade frequently. Serve with rice.

Per serving: *384kcals, 22.5g fat (10.4g saturated), 2.3g sugars, 23.9g protein, 1.9g fibre, 0.5g sodium*

DF

Lemon chicken with broccoli pesto

Serves 4

Zest and juice of 2 lemons
4 chicken fillets
1 head of broccoli, chopped into florets
25g (1/4 cup) Parmesan cheese
1 garlic clove

1. Whisk together half of the lemon zest, half of the lemon juice and one tablespoon of olive oil. Season the chicken with salt and pepper and place it in a baking dish. Pour over the lemon marinade and refrigerate for at least 30 minutes.

2. Bring a saucepan of water to the boil and cook the broccoli for four minutes until tender but still bright green.

3. Transfer the broccoli to a food processor and add the Parmesan, garlic and the rest of the lemon zest and juice. Pulse until the broccoli is chopped. Stream in more oil while the processor is running until the pesto is smooth.

4. Heat a grill pan over a medium-high heat and cook the chicken for about 3-4 minutes per side until cooked through. Slice the chicken into strips and top with the broccoli pesto to serve.

Per serving: *353kcals, 5.6g fat (2.1g saturated), 3g carbohydrates, 0.7g sugars, 48.7g protein, 0.6g fibre, 0.36g sodium*

LF DF GF

Low-fat butter chicken

Serves 4

800g (28oz) chicken thigh fillets, trimmed and cut into cubes
2 garlic cloves, crushed
2cm (1 inch) piece of fresh ginger, peeled and grated
½ tsp chilli powder
2 tsp garam masala
1 tsp ground cumin
1 tsp ground coriander (cilantro)
120g (½ cup) natural low-fat yoghurt
2 tsp vegetable oil
1 tsp ground cardamom
1 cinnamon stick
250g (1 cup) tomato purée
180ml (¾ cup) double cream

To serve:
Steamed basmati rice
Fresh coriander (cilantro) leaves

1. Combine chicken, garlic, ginger, chilli, garam masala, cumin, ground coriander and yoghurt in a bowl. Cover and leave to marinate for at least 15 minutes.

2. Heat the oil in a frying pan over a medium-high heat. Add the cardamom and cinnamon stick. Cook for one minute or until fragrant.

3. Add the chicken mixture. Cook, stirring, for 5-6 minutes or until browned.

4. Add tomato purée and 125ml (½ cup) of cold water. Bring to the boil. Reduce the heat to medium-low. Simmer, stirring occasionally, for 30 minutes.

5. Remove and discard the cinnamon stick. Add the cream and cook for two minutes or until heated through.

6. Divide the rice between bowls, top with the chicken mixture and a sprinkling of coriander to serve.

Per serving: *442kcals, 25.1g fat (9.9g saturated), 15.6g carbohydrates, 9.5g sugars, 38.3g protein, 4.6g fibre, 0.35g sodium*

DF

Roast chicken with vegetables

Serves 4

1.5kg (3.3lb) chicken, quartered
Salt and black pepper
1 lemon, halved
3 tbsp olive oil
450g (16oz) new potatoes, halved
115g (2 cups) radishes, halved
3 spring onions (scallions), cut into thirds
450g (16oz) carrots
Handful of fresh dill, chopped

1. Preheat the oven to 240˚C/ 220˚C fan/gas mark 9/460˚F. Rinse the chicken and pat dry with kitchen paper. Season with salt and pepper and place skin-side up on a baking tray.

2. Squeeze half of the lemon over the chicken and drizzle with one tablespoon of olive oil. Cook for 15 minutes.

3. Toss the potatoes, radishes, spring onion and carrots with the remaining two tablespoons of olive oil. Season with salt and pepper.

4. Remove the chicken from the oven and scatter the vegetables around it. Continue to cook for 20 minutes, or until the vegetables are tender and the chicken is golden and cooked through.

5. Squeeze the remaining lemon over the chicken and vegetables. Top with dill and season with salt.

Per serving: *316kcals, 14.3g fat (3.5g saturated), 2.6g carbohydrates, 0.6g sugars, 42.4g protein, 0g fibre, 0.1g sodium*

LF DF GF

Roasted curry chicken thighs with yoghurt cumin sauce

Serves 4

2 tsp cumin
4 garlic cloves, crushed
3 tbsp red Thai curry paste
285g (1 cup) Greek-style yoghurt
1kg (2.2lb) chicken thighs

1. Whisk together half of the cumin, half of the garlic and all of the curry paste. Stir in half of the yoghurt and transfer to a re-sealable plastic bag. Add the chicken and make sure all of the meat is covered in the marinade. Leave overnight or for up to 24 hours to marinate.

2. Preheat the oven to 220°C/200°C fan/gas mark 7/425°F. Remove the chicken from the marinade and pat dry with kitchen paper.

3. Bake on a tray for 30-35 minutes or until cooked through.

4. In a small bowl, whisk the remaining yoghurt, garlic and cumin and serve with the chicken.

Per serving: *575kcals, 25.6g fat (5.1g saturated), 5.8g carbohydrates, 0g sugars, 75.6g protein, 0g fibre, 0.37g sodium*

DF

Summer-stuffed chicken

Serves 4

170g (1 cup) artichoke hearts, drained and chopped
2 tbsp Parmesan, grated
2 tbsp fresh thyme, chopped
4 chicken breast fillets
2 tbsp plus 1 tsp extra virgin olive oil
Salt and black pepper
2 beef (beefsteak) tomatoes, chopped
1 shallot, thinly sliced
1 tbsp red wine vinegar

To serve:
Toasted baguette slices

1. Combine the artichokes, Parmesan and half of the thyme in a bowl. Cut a 5cm (2 inch) pocket in the thickest part of each chicken breast and stuff a quarter of the artichoke mixture into each pocket.

2. Rub the chicken breasts with one teaspoon of the oil and season with salt and pepper.

3. Heat a grill to medium and cook the chicken for seven minutes per side, until cooked through.

4. Mix the tomatoes, shallot, vinegar, remaining oil and thyme in a large bowl and season with salt and pepper.

5. Slice the chicken and serve warm with the tomato salad and baguette slices.

Per serving: *301kcals, 13.2g fat (3g saturated), 7g carbohydrates, 3g sugars, 38g protein, 1g fibre, 0.07g sodium*

LF DF

Thai turkey mince

Serves 4

1 tbsp peanut oil
750g (26.5oz) minced turkey
2 garlic cloves, crushed
1 small red chilli, finely chopped
5 tbsp (1/3 cup) sweet chilli sauce
Juice of 3 limes
1 red (Spanish) onion, halved and finely sliced
A handful of fresh coriander (cilantro) leaves, roughly chopped
4 iceberg lettuce leaves, shredded

To serve:
Boiled/steamed rice
Lime wedges

1. Heat the oil in a large non-stick frying pan over medium-high heat.

2. Add the mince, garlic and chilli and cook, stirring constantly, for 4-5 minutes or until mince is browned and cooked through. Transfer to a large bowl.

3. Add the sweet chilli sauce, lime juice, onion, coriander and lettuce to the mince and toss to combine. Serve with rice and lime wedges.

Per serving: *386kcals, 16.6g fat (0.6g saturated fat), 13g carbohydrates, 1.5g sugars, 43.6g protein, 0.8g fibre, 0g sodium*

LF DF

Turkey burgers with sweet potato chips

Serves 4

For the sweet potato chips:

4 sweet potatoes, scrubbed and cut into large chips
2 tbsp olive oil
Salt and black pepper

For the turkey burgers:

1 tbsp olive oil
1 onion, finely chopped
1 garlic clove, crushed
500g (18oz) minced turkey
Zest of 1 lemon
1 tsp dried thyme
A large handful of fresh flat-leaf parsley, chopped
4 burger buns
A handful of lettuce leaves
1 beef (beefsteak) tomato, sliced
2-4 tbsp tomato relish (or other dressing of your choice)

1. Heat the oven to 200°C/180°C fan/gas mark 6/400°F. In a large bowl, toss the sweet potato with oil and season with salt and pepper.

2. Transfer to a roasting tin and place in the oven to bake for 30-40 minutes, until crisp.

3. Meanwhile, heat the oil in a large non-stick frying pan over a medium heat. Add the onion and garlic and cook for 2-3 minutes until soft. Remove from the heat and allow to cool.

4. Add the turkey mince into a large bowl with the lemon zest, thyme, parsley and the softened onion and garlic. Season well with salt and pepper. Use clean hands to mix together until well combined.

5. Shape the mixture into four balls and flatten to form burgers. Place in a roasting tin, leaving space between each, and bake in the oven for 20-25 minutes.

6. Halve the buns and toast under the grill (or on a grill pan) until lightly golden.

7. Serve each burger on a bun with lettuce, sliced tomato, relish and a portion of sweet potato chips on the side.

Per serving: *618kcals, 18.9g fat (3.9g saturated), 67.1g carbohydrates, 5.3g sugars, 43.7g protein, 8g fibre, 0.32g sodium*

LF DF

Fabulous fowl

Chicken Caesar salad

Serves 4

1 medium crusty bread loaf
3 tbsp olive oil
2 skinless chicken breasts
1 large cos lettuce

For the dressing:
1 garlic clove
2 anchovies
Parmesan, for grating and garnish
5 tbsp mayonnaise
1 tbsp white wine vinegar

1. Heat the oven to 200°C/fan 180°C/gas mark 6/400°F. Tear the bread into big croutons or, if you prefer, cut with a knife. Spread over a large baking sheet or tray and sprinkle over two tablespoons of olive oil. Rub the oil into the bread and season with a little salt if you like. Bake for 8-10 minutes, turning the croutons a few times during cooking so they brown evenly.

2. Rub the chicken breasts with the remaining oil and season with salt and pepper. Place a pan over a medium heat for one minute, until hot but not smoking. Lay the chicken into the pan, it will sizzle if it's hot enough, and cook for four minutes. Turn the chicken and cook for a further four minutes. Check if it's cooked by poking the tip of a sharp knife into the thickest part; there should be no sign of pink and juices will run clear.

3. Crush the garlic and mash the anchovies with a fork against the side of a small bowl. Grate a handful of Parmesan and mix with the rest of the dressing ingredients. Season to taste. It should be the consistency of yoghurt – if yours is thicker, stir in a few teaspoons of water to thin it.

4. Shave the Parmesan with a peeler. Tear lettuce into large pieces and put in a large bowl. Pull chicken into bite-size strips and scatter half over the leaves, along with half the croutons. Add most of the dressing and toss with your fingers. Scatter the rest of the chicken and croutons and then drizzle with the remaining dressing. Sprinkle the Parmesan on top and serve straight away.

Per serving: *443kcals, 32.65g fat (1.35g saturated), 19.25g carbohydrates, 0.65g sugars, 19.4g protein, 0.82g fibre, 0.3g sodium*

LF DF

Chilli lime chicken

Serves 4

Juice of 2 limes
2 tbsp vegetable oil
1 tbsp white wine
1 tsp ground cumin
Salt and black pepper
1 jalapeño pepper, deseeded and sliced
600g (21oz) chicken fillets

To serve:
Brown rice, cooked to packet instructions
A small handful of fresh coriander (cilantro) leaves, chopped
Lime juice

1. Whisk the lime juice, oil, wine, cumin and a pinch of salt and pepper in a bowl. Stir in the jalapeño pepper.

2. Place the chicken in a baking dish and pour over the marinade. Cover with cling film (plastic wrap) and refrigerate for at least 30 minutes.

3. Heat a grill pan to a medium-high heat and cook the chicken for four minutes per side, or until cooked through. Leave to cool slightly and slice into thick strips.

4. Toss the cooked brown rice with the coriander leaves and lime juice and serve with the chicken strips.

Per serving: *532kcals, 19.4g fat (4.7g saturated), 39.2g carbohydrates, 0g sugars, 47.3g protein, 1.9g fibre, 0.13g sodium*

LF DF GF

Crispy chicken with broccoli slaw

Serves 4

1 tsp olive oil, for greasing
1 tsp paprika
310ml (1¼ cups) buttermilk
Salt and black pepper
4 chicken breasts
8 cream (savoury) crackers, crushed
80g (¾ cup) breadcrumbs
4 tbsp (¼ cup) mayonnaise
1 tbsp cider vinegar
1 head of broccoli, cut into florets
2 carrots, grated
2 spring onions (scallions), chopped

1. Preheat the oven to 190°C/170°C fan/gas mark 5/375°F. Lightly grease a baking tray with oil and line with parchment paper.

2. In a large bowl, combine the paprika and 250ml (1 cup) of buttermilk, season with salt and pepper. Add the chicken and turn to coat in the mixture.

3. Combine the crackers and breadcrumbs in another bowl. Dip each piece of chicken into the cracker mixture and toss to coat.

4. Place the chicken onto the prepared baking tray and bake in the oven for 35-40 minutes until the chicken is cooked through and golden and crispy.

5. Meanwhile, put a large saucepan of water over a high heat and bring to the boil. Add the broccoli and cook for 2-3 minutes. Remove from the heat, drain and rinse under cold water to stop the cooking process. Set aside.

6. In a large bowl, whisk together the mayonnaise, vinegar and remaining buttermilk, season with salt and pepper.

7. Add the broccoli, carrot and spring onion and toss to combine. Serve with the chicken.

Per serving: *531kcals, 15.6g fat (3.7g saturated), 56.2g carbohydrates, 10.1g sugars, 42.9g protein, 7.8g fibre, 0.6g sodium*

LF

Easy chicken pad Thai

Serves 4

250g (9oz) rice noodles
2 limes, juiced
2 tbsp fish sauce
2 tbsp brown sugar
2 tbsp peanut oil
4 chicken breast fillets, thinly sliced
3 spring onions (scallions), thinly sliced
2 red chillies, de-seeded, finely chopped
1 handful of bean sprouts
3 tbsp roasted peanuts, chopped (optional)
1 handful of coriander (cilantro) leaves

To serve:
Lime wedges

1. Pop the noodles into a large heat-proof bowl. Cover with hot water and leave to stand until tender. Drain and rinse under cold water.

2. Combine the lime juice, fish sauce and sugar in a small bowl and whisk to combine.

3. Heat a wok over a high heat. Add the oil, swirling to coat the whole base. Add the chicken and stir-fry until golden. Add the spring onions, chillies and bean sprouts. Stir-fry for two to three minutes. Add the noodles and the sauce and stir-fry for a further two minutes.

4. Spoon onto plates, sprinkle with coriander leaves and peanuts (if using). Finish with a wedge of lime and serve!

Per serving: *482kcals, 10.9g fat (2.2g saturated), 57.1g carbohydrates, 5.72g sugars, 31.1g protein 0.01g fibre, 0.49 sodium*

LF DF

Greek-style chicken skewers

Serves 4

4 chicken breasts, chopped into bite-sized chunks
2½ tbsp olive oil
1 lemon, juiced
2 garlic cloves, crushed
1 tsp dried oregano
100g (3.5oz) Feta, cut into cubes
200g (7oz) cherry tomatoes, halved
Handful of black olives, halved
1 x 400g (14oz) can cannellini beans, drained
Handful of rocket (arugula)
Skewers, soaked in water

1. Thread the chicken onto skewers and place into a dish. Combine 2 tablespoons of olive oil, 2 tablespoons of lemon juice, the garlic and oregano and pour over the chicken. Refrigerate for at least half an hour.

2. Combine the Feta, tomatoes, olives, beans and rocket in a bowl. Drizzle with lemon juice and oil. Season and toss.

3. Heat a griddle and cook the chicken for 3 minutes on each side or until cooked through. Serve with the Feta bean salad.

Per serving: *548kcals, 15g fat (4g saturated), 51g carbohydrates, 5.1g sugars, 54g protein, 22.8g fibre, 0.6g sodium*

LF DF GF

Grilled turkey with mint pesto

Serves 4

4 turkey steaks (about 150g/5.5oz each)
4 tbsp lemon juice
Salt and pepper

For the mint pesto:
Small handful of fresh mint leaves
25g (3 tbsp) hazelnuts, skinned and roughly chopped
1-2 garlic cloves
7 tbsp olive oil
Zest and juice of 1 lemon
2 tbsp grated Parmesan

To serve:
Mint sprigs
Lemon wedges

1. Preheat the grill to high. Make three or four cuts in the turkey steak, sprinkle with 2 tablespoons of lemon juice and leave aside while you make the pesto.

2. Blend together the mint leaves, hazelnuts, garlic cloves and one tablespoon of the oil in a food processor for 1-2 minutes. Gradually pour in more of the oil until you have a smooth pesto. Spoon the mixture into a bowl and stir in the lemon juice and zest, Parmesan and seasoning.

3. Spoon some of the pesto over the turkey and grill for three minutes on each side. Reduce the heat to medium and cook for another 10-15 minutes on each side (depending on thickness) until cooked through, brushing occasionally with the pesto. Pour over the remaining lemon juice and serve with mint sprigs and lemon wedges.

Per serving: *547kcals, 35.1g fat (6.4g saturated), 1.7g carbohydrates, 1.1g sugars, 57g protein, 0g fibre, 0.3g sodium*

DF GF

Honey mustard chicken thighs

Serves 4

8-10 chicken thighs
4 tbsp (¼ cup) wholegrain mustard
4 tbsp (¼ cup) honey
Salt and pepper

To serve:
Mashed potatoes

1. Preheat the oven to 180°C/160°C fan/gas mark 5/350°F.

2. In a large bowl, mix together the mustard, honey and seasoning. Add the chicken thighs and toss to coat. Transfer the chicken to a single layer in a roasting tin.

3. Cook for 25-30 minutes, basting with the juices once or twice throughout, until cooked through and the juices run clear. Serve with mashed potatoes.

Per serving: *462kcals, 29g fat (7.5g saturated), 12g carbohydrates, 12g sugars, 39g protein, 0g fibre, 0.5g sodium*

Chicken tandoori pizza

Serves 4

150g (2/3 cup) Greek natural yoghurt
1 tbsp tandoori curry powder
450g (16oz) chicken breast fillets, cut into small pieces
2 tbsp olive oil
½ red (Spanish) onion, thinly sliced
4 naan breads
200g (7oz) pineapple, chopped
100g (3.5oz) Mozzarella, shredded
A handful of fresh coriander (cilantro) leaves, chopped

1. Stir together the yoghurt and curry powder in a large bowl. Add the chicken and toss to combine.

2. Preheat the oven to 200°C/180°C fan/gas mark 6/400°F. Heat the oil in a frying pan over a medium-low heat and cook the onion for 10 minutes until soft.

3. Add the chicken and marinade and cook for 5-7 minutes until cooked through.

4. Remove from the heat and spoon the chicken over each of the naan breads. Top with the onions, pineapple and Mozzarella.

5. Bake for 8-10 minutes until the cheese melts. Top with fresh coriander to serve.

Per serving: *683kcals, 29.6g fat (6.5g saturated), 49.2g carbohydrates, 5.7g sugars, 52g protein, 3.4g fibre, 0.27g sodium*

DF

Paprika chicken

Serves 4

1 whole chicken, cut into 4-6 pieces
Salt and black pepper
1 tbsp olive oil
1 onion, halved and thinly sliced
2 garlic cloves, thinly sliced
1 tbsp sweet paprika
2 tsp fennel seeds
4 tomatoes, diced
470ml (2 cups) chicken stock
75g (1/3 cup) sour cream
A large handful of fresh flat-leaf parsley, finely chopped

To serve:
Rice or potatoes

1. Season the chicken with salt and pepper.

2. Heat oil in a large heavy-based saucepan over a medium heat. Cook the chicken for 3-4 minutes each side or until golden, you may have to do this in batches. Transfer cooked chicken to a plate lined with kitchen paper.

3. Add the onion and garlic to the pan. Cook, stirring, for 2-3 minutes or until soft.

4. Add the paprika and fennel seeds. Cook, stirring, for one minute.

5. Stir in tomato and stock.

6. Add the chicken and bring to the boil. Reduce the heat to low, cover and simmer for 50 minutes. Uncover and simmer for a further 25 minutes. Remove from the heat.

7. Stir in the sour cream, sprinkle with parsley and serve.

Per serving: *504kcals, 16.7g fat (5.7g saturated), 10.7g carbohydrates, 4.9g sugars, 75.3g protein, 3g fibre, 0.5g sodium*

DF

Turkey pilaf

Serves 2-3

2 tbsp olive oil
1 onion, finely chopped
Pinch of chilli flakes
150g (5.5 oz) long-grain rice
2 carrots, chopped
2 garlic cloves, chopped
1 tsp ground cumin
1 tsp dried oregano
1 x 400g (14oz) can chopped tomatoes
600ml (2½ cups) chicken or turkey stock
200g (7oz) frozen peas
350g (12oz) cooked turkey, chopped or shredded
Salt and pepper

To serve:
Handful of fresh coriander (cilantro)

1. Heat oil in a large frying pan. Add the onion and sauté for 3-4 minutes or until softened. Add the rice, chilli flakes and chopped carrots and cook for a further 1-2 minutes.

2. Pour in the chopped tomatoes, garlic, cumin, oregano and stock. Bring to the boil then reduce to a simmer and leave to cook for 20 minutes, stirring frequently.

3. Stir in the frozen peas and shredded turkey and cook for a further 8-10 minutes until both are cooked through. Season and serve with a sprinkling of fresh coriander.

Per serving: *522kcals, 14.8g fat (2.5g saturated), 64.1g carbohydrates, 12.3g sugars, 37.2g protein, 6.3g fibre, 1.7g sodium*

LF

Low-fat 30-minute meals

Cajun chicken penne

Serves 6

450g (16oz) penne
4 chicken breasts, sliced into thin strips
1 tbsp Cajun seasoning
Cooking spray
2 green peppers (capsicums), chopped
1 red pepper (capsicum), chopped
8 mushrooms, sliced
2 spring onions (scallions), finely chopped
2 garlic cloves, crushed
700ml (3 cups) cream
½ tsp dried basil
Salt and black pepper
20g (3½ tbsp) Parmesan, grated
1 lime, cut into 4 wedges

1. Bring a large saucepan of water to the boil and cook the penne according to the package instructions.

2. Toss the chicken with the Cajun seasoning until coated. Squirt some cooking spray into a frying pan over a medium heat and cook the chicken for seven minutes until thoroughly cooked.

3. Add the peppers, mushrooms, spring onions and garlic and cook for three minutes.

4. Reduce the heat and stir in the cream. Season with basil, salt and pepper then add the penne. Sprinkle with Parmesan and serve with the lime wedges.

Per serving: *821kcals, 46.8g fat (25.5g saturated), 42.6g carbohydrates, 2.7g sugars, 45.4g protein, 9.7g fibre, 0.22g sodium*

DF

Chilli burgers

Serves 4

500g (17.5oz) minced beef
1 red chilli, deseeded and finely chopped
2 tbsp dried coriander (cilantro)
Salt and black pepper
1 tbsp olive oil
A small handful of lettuce leaves (any type)
4 burger buns, toasted

For the salsa:
300g (10.5oz) cherry tomatoes
Juice of 1 lime
2 tbsp sweet chilli sauce
1 small red (Spanish) onion, finely chopped
2 tsp dried coriander (cilantro)

1. In a large bowl, add the minced beef, chilli and coriander, season well with salt and pepper. Using your hands (making sure they are clean), mix everything together and form four burger patties, about 2.5cm (1 inch) thick.

2. To make the salsa, add all of the ingredients into a small bowl and mix together. Blitz together with a hand blender for a few seconds.

3. Heat one tablespoon of oil in a non-stick frying pan on a medium-high heat. Add the burgers and cook on each side for 4-5 minutes or until cooked to your liking.

4. To serve, place 1-2 lettuce leaves on the bottom half of a burger bun, add a burger and top with some salsa and the top of the bun.

Per serving: *438kcals, 12.9g fat (3.8g saturated), 35.5g carbohydrates, 5.4g sugars, 42.8g protein, 3.1g fibre, 0.4g sodium*

LF DF

Chilli maple pork

Serves 4

1 tsp chilli powder
A pinch of salt
500g (17.5oz) pork tenderloin, trimmed and cut crosswise into 3cm (1.5 inch) thick medallions
2 tsp vegetable oil
60ml (1/4 cup) apple cider
1 tbsp maple syrup
1 tsp cider vinegar

1. Mix the chilli powder and salt and rub over the pork medallions.

2. Heat the oil in a large frying pan over a medium-high heat. Add the pork and cook for two minutes per side.

3. Stir in the cider, syrup and vinegar and bring to the boil, using the spoon to scrape up any bits from the bottom.

4. Reduce the heat to medium and cook for an additional three minutes until the sauce is reduced to a thick glaze, turning the pork occasionally to coat.

5. Serve the pork warm, drizzled with the glaze.

Per serving: *222kcals, 6.8g fat (2g saturated), 5.6g carbohydrates, 4.8g sugars, 32.8g protein, 0g fibre, 0.12g sodium*

LF DF GF

Ginger pork stir-fry

Serves 2

1 tbsp olive oil
250g (9oz) pork, cut into strips
3cm (1.5 inch) piece of fresh root ginger, grated
1 garlic clove, crushed
1 red pepper (capsicum), cut into strips
2-3 spring onions (scallions), sliced
1 small red chilli, diced
2 tsp soy sauce
1 tsp sesame oil
1 tbsp white wine or rice vinegar
Salt and pepper
300g (10oz) noodles
Handful of fresh coriander (cilantro), to garnish

1. Heat a wok or large pan until very hot. Add the oil and swirl in the pan until well coated. Add the pork strips and stir-fry for 3-4 minutes before adding in the ginger, garlic, pepper, spring onions and chilli and cooking for another minute.

2. In a separate bowl, mix together the soy sauce, sesame oil, vinegar, salt and pepper. Pour over the stir-fry before adding in the noodles.

3. Toss all ingredients together until well combined and cook for 2-3 minutes until the noodles are cooked through. Top with the coriander and serve.

Per serving: *322 kcals, 15.3g fat (3g saturated), 18.6g carbohydrates, 4.8g sugars, 28.4g protein, 2.3g fibre, 0.55g sodium*

LF DF

Harissa lamb chops with Feta

Serves 4

4 lamb gigot chops (or 8 small centre loin chops)
1½ tbsp harissa paste
400g (14oz) rocket (arugula)
1 red (Spanish) onion, grated
A small handful of flat-leaf parsley, chopped
100g (3.5oz) Feta, crumbled

For the tzatziki dressing:
1 garlic clove, finely chopped
A handful of fresh mint leaves, finely chopped
200g (7oz) Greek-style yoghurt
Salt and black pepper

To serve:
4 crusty bread rolls

1. Heat the grill to high. Place the lamb chops on a grill pan and spread some harissa paste on top of each.
2. Place under the grill and cook for four minutes on each side or until cooked to your liking, spreading more paste on the underside when it is turned over.
3. Add the tzatziki ingredients into a bowl and mix together. Add a little drop of water to make it more of a dressing consistency.
4. In a salad bowl, add the rocket, red onion, parsley and Feta. Toss together.
5. Drizzle the salad with some tzatziki dressing.
6. Serve each lamb chop with some salad and more tzatziki on the side, plus a crusty roll.

Per serving: *340kcals, 16g fat (6.5g saturated), 13.2g carbohydrates, 4.9g sugars, 34.9g protein, 2.2g fibre, 0.5g sodium*

DF

High protein Greek-style chicken burgers

Serves 4

400g (14oz) chicken mince
3 tbsp fresh coriander (cilantro) leaves, chopped
2 tbsp breadcrumbs
60g (2oz) Feta, crumbled
Salt and black pepper
1 tbsp balsamic vinegar
2 tbsp olive oil
1 tsp dried oregano
1 tomato, thickly sliced
1 red (Spanish) onion, thickly sliced

To serve:
2 whole-wheat pita breads, halved
4 tbsp hummus
Rocket (arugula) leaves

1. Mix the chicken mince, coriander, breadcrumbs, Feta and a pinch of salt and pepper together. Shape into four patties.

2. Whisk together the vinegar, oil and oregano in a large bowl. Add the tomatoes and onions and toss to coat.

3. Coat a barbecue or grill pan with cooking spray. Cook the patties for 10 minutes, flipping once, until cooked through then set aside.

4. Add the tomato and onion slices to the barbecue or grill pan and cook for 6-8 minutes, flipping once, until charred and tender.

5. Spread the inside of each pita with hummus and fill with rocket leaves, a burger, tomatoes and onion.

Per serving: *380kcals, 20.7g fat (5.9g saturated), 26.1g carbohydrates, 2.4g sugars, 29.8g protein, 4.3g fibre, 0.47g sodium*

DF

Mexican chilli pork

Serves 6

Cooking spray
600g (21oz) pork fillet, cut into bite-size pieces
½ an onion, chopped
2 tsp chilli powder
1 tsp ground cumin
½ tsp ground cinnamon
2 x 400g (14oz) cans chopped tomatoes
50g (⅓ cup) plain chocolate, chopped

To serve:
Rice

1. Coat a large frying pan with cooking spray and heat over a medium-high heat. Add the pork and cook for five minutes, stirring occasionally, until cooked through. Remove from the pan and set aside.

2. Add the onion and cook for three minutes until soft. Add the chilli powder, cumin and cinnamon. Cook for one minute until fragrant, stirring frequently.

3. Add the tomatoes and chocolate and bring to the boil. Reduce the heat to medium-low, cover and cook for eight minutes. Return the meat to the mixture and serve warm over cooked rice.

Per serving: *340kcals, 17.7g fat (7.5g saturated), 15.3g carbohydrates, 10.4g sugars, 30g protein, 3.4g fibre, 0.05g sodium*

Pork and almond stir fry

Serves 4

400g (14oz) pork fillet, thinly sliced
2 red (Spanish) onions, cut into wedges
1 tbsp fresh ginger, finely grated
½ tsp Chinese five-spice
1 tbsp vegetable oil
25g (¼ cup) almonds
1 punnet baby corn, halved
8 tbsp (½ cup) oyster sauce
200g (7oz) thin egg noodles

1. Add the pork, onion, ginger and five spice into a large bowl and stir well to combine. Set aside.

2. Heat half the vegetable oil in a wok over a high heat. Add the almonds and stir-fry for two minutes or until golden. Transfer to a bowl.

3. Add one-quarter of the pork mixture and stir-fry for 1-2 minutes or until golden. Transfer to a bowl. Repeat, in batches, with the remaining mixture until all of it is cooked.

4. Heat the remaining oil in the wok over a high heat. Add the baby corn and stir-fry for 1-2 minutes or until tender.

5. Add the pork, almonds and oyster sauce and stir-fry for 1-2 minutes until heated through.

6. Meanwhile, place a large saucepan of water over a high heat and bring to the boil. Add the noodles and cook as per packet instructions. Drain well.

7. Divide the noodles evenly among serving bowls and top with the pork stir-fry. Serve immediately.

Per serving: *605kcals, 26.4g fat (6.6g saturated), 53g carbohydrates, 5.1g sugars, 40.1g protein, 5.6g fibre, 0.29g sodium*

DF

Steak pizzaiola

Serves 4

600g (21oz) sirloin steak, excess fat trimmed
Salt and black pepper
2 tbsp olive oil
4 garlic cloves, crushed
1 onion, sliced
1 yellow pepper (capsicum), deseeded and sliced
1 red pepper (capsicum), deseeded and sliced
1 x 400g (14oz) can chopped tomatoes
½ tsp dried oregano
A pinch of chilli flakes
2 tbsp fresh parsley leaves, chopped

To serve:
Focaccia bread

1. Season the steak with salt and black pepper. Heat the oil in a large frying pan over a high heat. Add the steak and cook for two minutes per side until well-browned. Transfer to a plate.

2. Add the garlic, onion and peppers to the pan and cook for four minutes until soft.

3. Stir in the tomatoes, oregano, chilli flakes and 150ml (½ cup plus 1 tbsp) of water. Bring to a simmer then add the steaks and cook for about 7-9 minutes for medium rare.

4. Transfer the steaks to a board to rest for five minutes. Simmer the sauce for another few minutes until thick.

5. Thinly slice the steak and divide among four plates. Top with the sauce and parsley. Serve with focaccia.

Per serving: *395kcals, 16.8g fat (4.6g saturated), 12.4g carbohydrates, 5g sugars, 47.7g protein, 3g fibre, 0.1g sodium*

LF

Thai pork and noodle soup

Serves 4

2 tbsp vegetable oil
2 spring onions (scallions), thinly sliced, white and green parts separated
2 garlic cloves, chopped
1 tbsp fresh ginger, grated
400g (14oz) pork mince
120g (1½ cups) mushrooms, thinly sliced
1L (4 cups) chicken stock
1 tbsp soy sauce
100g (3.5oz) rice noodles
Juice of ½ a lime

To serve:
Fresh coriander (cilantro) leaves, chopped
Lime wedges

1. Heat the oil in a large saucepan over a medium-high heat. Add the spring onion whites, garlic and ginger and cook, stirring, for 30 seconds.

2. Add the pork and cook, breaking it up with a spoon, for 6-8 minutes until browned and cooked through. Add the mushrooms and cook for three more minutes.

3. Add the stock, soy sauce and 500ml (2 cups) of water to the saucepan and bring to the boil. Add the noodles, reduce the heat and simmer until tender. Stir in the lime juice. Serve with the spring onion greens, coriander and lime wedges.

Per serving: *394kcals, 11.7g fat (1.5g saturated), 73g carbohydrates, 1.9g sugars, 3.1g protein, 2.2g fibre, 1.1g sodium*

LF DF

Perfect sides

Balsamic grilled beetroot and quinoa salad

Serves 4

200g (7oz) beetroot, peeled, quartered and thickly sliced
2 tbsp balsamic vinegar
300g (1¾ cup) quinoa
60g (¼ cup) applesauce
Salt and black pepper
60g (½ cup) goat's cheese, crumbled

To serve:
40g (2 cups) rocket (arugula)

1. Toss the beetroot with the vinegar and leave to marinate for 15 minutes.

2. Heat a grill pan to a medium high heat and cook the beetroot for 20-25 minutes, flipping once, until cooked through.

3. Meanwhile, bring a large saucepan of water to the boil and cook the quinoa according to the packet instructions.

4. Heat a small saucepan over a low heat and stir in the applesauce and one tablespoon of water.

5. Drain the quinoa, toss with the applesauce mixture and season with salt and pepper.

6. Remove the beetroot from the heat. Arrange the quinoa on the plates and top with the rocket and the goat's cheese. Arrange the beetroot on top and season with salt and pepper. Serve warm.

Per serving: *406kcals, 12.6g fat (6g saturated), 54.9g carbohydrates, 5.6g sugars, 18.4g protein, 6.4g fibre, 0.18g sodium*

LF

Chickpea patties with Greek salad

Serves 4

1 x 400g (14oz) can chickpeas, rinsed and drained
A handful of fresh parsley, chopped
1 garlic clove, crushed
½ tsp ground cumin
Salt and black pepper
2 tbsp flour
2 tbsp olive oil
150g (½ cup) Greek natural yoghurt
Juice of 1 lemon

For the salad:
65g (⅓ cup) pitted black olives, halved
1 cucumber, halved lengthwise and sliced
½ red (Spanish) onion, thinly sliced
1 tomato, cubed
60g (½ cup) Feta, crumbled
1 tbsp extra virgin olive oil
½ tbsp balsamic vinegar
½ tsp dried oregano

1. Combine the chickpeas, parsley, garlic, cumin and a pinch of salt and pepper in a food processor and pulse until the mixture comes together. Shape into eight patties and coat in the flour.

2. Heat the oil in a frying pan over a medium-high heat and cook the patties for 5-7 minutes, flipping once.

3. Whisk together the yoghurt and lemon juice and refrigerate until needed.

4. Combine the olives, cucumbers, onion and tomato in a bowl. Add the Feta and toss gently.

5. Whisk the oil, vinegar and oregano and pour over the salad, tossing to coat.

6. Serve the patties with a drizzle of the yoghurt mixture and the salad on the side.

Per serving: *406kcals, 17g fat (4.1g saturated), 48.9g carbohydrates, 9.3g sugars, 17.4g protein, 12.7g fibre, 0.32g sodium*

LF

Couscous salad with peas and mint

Serves 4

470ml (2 cups) vegetable stock
260g (1½ cups) couscous
145g (1 cup) peas
3 spring onions (scallions), thinly sliced
A handful of fresh mint, chopped
Juice of 1 lemon
4 tbsp (¼ cup) olive oil
Salt and black pepper

1. Bring the vegetable stock to the boil in a large saucepan over a medium heat. Stir in the couscous and remove from the heat. Allow to sit for 5-7 minutes or until the stock is absorbed. Fluff with a fork.

2. Bring a saucepan of water to the boil and cook the peas for three minutes, until bright green and tender. Rinse in cold water and allow them to cool.

3. Whisk together the lemon juice and olive oil and season generously with salt and pepper.

4. When the couscous is cool, add the peas, mint and spring onions and coat with the dressing. Serve immediately or store to let the flavours combine.

Per serving: *398kcals, 14.4g fat (2g saturated), 55.8g carbohydrates, 3.3g sugars, 10.7g protein, 6g fibre, 0.07g sodium*

LF DF

Lentil and squash salad

Serves 4

450g (16oz) butternut squash, peeled and cubed
Olive oil
Salt and black pepper
230ml (1 cup) apple juice
145g (¾ cup) puy lentils
80g (4 cups) rocket (arugula)
40g (⅓ cup) Feta, crumbled

1. Preheat the oven to 200°C/180°C fan/gas mark 6/400°F. Toss the butternut squash with a drizzle of olive oil and a pinch of salt and pepper on a baking tray. Cook for 20-30 minutes until the squash has browned on the edges.

2. Heat the apple juice and 80ml (⅓ cup) of water in a saucepan over a medium heat and cook the lentils for 20 minutes.

3. Drain off the lentils and return the liquid to the pan. Bring it to the boil then reduce the heat and simmer until it thickens into a dressing. Pour it into a mixing bowl and leave to cool.

4. Toss the rocket, squash and lentils with the dressing and transfer the whole mixture to a serving bowl. Add the Feta and toss gently to combine.

Per serving: *277kcals, 5.6g fat (3.1g saturated), 47.7g carbohydrates, 13.7g sugars, 13.6g protein, 8.9g fibre, 0.24g sodium*

GF

Marinated roasted peppers with capers and Mozzarella

Serves 6

3 red peppers (capsicums)
3 yellow peppers (capsicums)
1½ tbsp extra virgin olive oil
4 tbsp (¼ cup) balsamic vinegar
1 garlic clove, minced
Salt and black pepper
2 tbsp capers, drained
2 tbsp flat-leaf parsley, chopped
225g (8oz) Mozzarella, sliced

1. Preheat the oven to 200°C/180°C fan/gas mark 6/400°F. Rub the peppers with half of the oil and arrange on a baking tray. Cook for 45 minutes to one hour, rotating every 15 minutes until the skins are black.

2. Transfer the peppers to a glass bowl and cover with cling film (plastic wrap). Leave to cool then remove the skins and seeds from the peppers. Slice the flesh into thin strips.

3. Toss the peppers with the vinegar, garlic and a good pinch of salt. Cover and leave to marinate for at least 30 minutes (and for up to four days) in the fridge.

4. To serve, arrange the peppers on a plate and sprinkle over the capers and parsley. Arrange the Mozzarella around the peppers, drizzle with the remaining oil and season with salt and pepper.

Per serving: *181kcals, 11.2g fat (5.3g saturated), 9.8g carbohydrates, 1.5g sugars, 11.2g protein, 1.3g fibre, 0.29 sodium*

DF GF

Panzanella - Italian bread and tomato salad

Serves 4-6

120g (4 cups) stale or part-baked ciabatta bread, torn into large pieces
8 tbsp (½ cup) extra virgin olive oil
700g (3 cups) mixed tomatoes, roughly chopped
Salt and black pepper
A small handful of capers, drained and chopped
1 red (Spanish) onion, thinly sliced
1 x 280g (10oz) jar of roasted peppers, drained and chopped
2 tbsp balsamic vinegar
A large handful of fresh basil

1. Preheat the oven to 180°C/160°C fan/gas mark 4/350°F. Arrange the bread on a baking tray and toss with two tablespoons of olive oil, salt and pepper. Bake for 8-10 minutes, until the bread is crisp and lightly browned. Leave to cool slightly.

2. Season the tomatoes with salt and pepper and mix in the capers, onion, peppers and bread.

3. Stir in the vinegar and remaining oil and season with salt and pepper. Toss with the basil leaves and serve.

Per serving: *271kcals, 16.6g fat (2.3g saturated), 29.3g carbohydrates, 6.8g sugars, 4.6g protein, 3.3g fibre, 0.38g sodium*

LF DF

Roasted vegetable and couscous salad

Serves 4-6

2 courgettes (zucchinis), chopped
1 yellow pepper (capsicum), deseeded and cut into strips
1 red pepper (capsicum), deseeded and cut into strips
1 aubergine (eggplant), chopped
1 red (Spanish) onion, quartered
2 garlic cloves, whole
60ml (4 tbsp) olive oil, plus extra for drizzling
½ tsp dried mixed herbs
1 garlic clove, crushed
470ml (2 cups) chicken or vegetable stock
1 small head of broccoli, cut into small florets
260g (1½ cups) couscous
12-15 cherry tomatoes, halved
2 tbsp fresh parsley, chopped
Zest and juice of 1 lemon
Salt and pepper

1. Preheat the oven to 220°C/200°C fan/gas mark 7/425°F. Layer the courgettes, peppers, aubergine, red onion and whole garlic cloves in a baking dish, drizzle with olive oil and sprinkle over the mixed herbs. Toss to coat then roast in the oven for approximately 20-30 minutes, until the vegetables are tender.

2. Heat two tablespoons of the oil in a large saucepan and add the garlic. Pour in the stock and add the broccoli florets. Bring to the boil.

3. Reduce the heat slightly then pour in the couscous in a steady stream. Give the couscous a quick stir then cover and remove from the heat. Leave for 10 minutes to allow the stock to be absorbed.

4. Fluff the couscous with a fork and season. When the couscous is completely cold, transfer it to a large serving dish. Top with the roasted vegetables, cherry tomatoes and chopped parsley.

5. In a separate small bowl, combine the remaining olive oil, lemon juice and zest, pour over the couscous and toss when serving.

Per serving: *314 kcals, 10.5g fat, (1.5g saturated), 47.8g carbohydrates, 5.6g sugars, 9.5g protein, 7.3g fibre, 0.28g sodium*

Sesame noodle salad

Serves 4

300g (10.5oz) noodles
250g (1 cup) mangetout (snow peas), trimmed and diagonally sliced
8 tbsp (½ cup) reduced-sodium soy sauce
2 tbsp sesame oil
2 tbsp vegetable oil
2 tbsp lime juice
2 tsp chilli flakes
5 spring onions (scallions), chopped
A small handful of fresh coriander (cilantro) leaves, chopped
2 tbsp sesame seeds, toasted

1. Bring a large saucepan of water to the boil and cook the noodles according to the package instructions. Add the mangetout during the last four minutes of cooking. Drain and rinse under cold water.

2. Whisk together the soy sauce, sesame oil, vegetable oil, lime juice, chilli flakes, half of the spring onions and half of the coriander.

3. Toss with the noodles, mangetout and sesame seeds. Serve chilled or at room temperature with the remaining spring onions and coriander.

Per serving: *495 kcals, 36.1g fat (6gsaturated fat), 33.2g carbohydrates, 4.4g sugars, 12.1g protein, 4.4g fibre, 2.16 sodium*

LF DF

Summer salad with soft boiled eggs

Serves 4

8 eggs
2 tbsp red wine vinegar
1 tsp Dijon mustard
Salt and black pepper
2 tbsp olive oil
2 garlic cloves, thinly sliced
4 slices bread, crusts removed and cut into 2cm (1 inch)cubes
150g (5 cups) mixed salad leaves

1. Bring a saucepan of water to the boil. Cook the eggs for six minutes (for runny yolks) and allow to cool.

2. In a bowl, whisk together the vinegar, mustard, half of the oil and season with salt and pepper.

3. Heat the remaining oil in a large frying pan over a medium heat. Add the garlic and cook for one minute, or until golden, then transfer to a plate using a slotted spoon.

4. Add the bread cubes to the oil and cook, turning until golden.

5. Divide the salad leaves among the serving plates and sprinkle with the garlic and croutons. Crack the eggs, break them in half, and scoop them from the shells onto the salad with a spoon. Top with the vinaigrette and season with salt and pepper. Serve warm.

Per serving: *232kcals, 15.9g fat (3.7g saturated), 7.1g carbohydrates, 1.1g sugars, 11.9g protein, 0g fibre, 0.20g sodium*

LF DF

Toasted cauliflower salad

Serves 4

600g (21oz) cauliflower, cut into florets
1 tbsp olive oil
2 tsp ground cumin
1 tsp ground turmeric
1 tsp fennel seeds
½ tsp ground cinnamon
½ cup pine nuts, toasted
½ cup raisins
30g (1 cup) baby spinach
Salt and black pepper

1. Place the cauliflower in a saucepan of water and cook for 10 minutes or until just tender. Drain and set aside.

2. Heat a large frying pan over a medium-high heat and add the spices. Cook, stirring, for one minute or until they become fragrant.

3. Add the cauliflower to the spices and cook, stirring, for five minutes or until golden.

4. Remove from the heat and stir in the pine nuts, raisins and spinach. Season with salt and pepper.

Per serving: *285kcal, 18.3g fat (1.6g saturated), 29.9g carbohydrates, 16.3g sugars, 7.5g protein, 6.9g fibre, 0g sodium*

LF

One-pot wonders

Beef and Guinness stew

Serves 4

1kg (2.2lb) stewing beef
1 tbsp flour
25g (2 tbsp) butter
Olive oil
1 onion, chopped
2 garlic cloves, chopped
1 carrot, peeled and diced
1 celery stalk, diced
250ml (1 cup) Guinness
250ml (1 cup) beef stock
A good pinch of salt and a few grindings of fresh black pepper
1 bay leaf
Fresh thyme leaves, stripped from 4 stalks

1. Preheat the oven to 170°C/150°C fan/gas mark 3/325°F.

2. Melt the butter and a little olive oil in a large casserole dish or saucepan on the stove (make sure it can also be used in the oven). Add the salt and pepper to the flour mixture, stir and toss the beef in it. Take out the beef, shake and fry in the butter and oil until browned.

3. Remove the beef and set aside on a plate. Scrape up the bits from the bottom of the dish and add the onion, garlic, diced carrot and celery. Cover and cook for 8-10 minutes, stirring occasionally.

4. Add the beef, Guinness, stock, salt, pepper, bay leaf and thyme. Cover the casserole and bake in the oven until the meat is cooked – this can take between an hour and a half and two hours. You need to stir it a few times in between and add some boiling water to top it up if it needs more juice.

Per serving: *420kcals, 14.4g fat (6.9g saturated), 12.1g carbohydrates, 4.9g sugars, 58g protein, 0.5g fibre, 0.4g sodium*

DF

Chicken with tarragon

Serves 4

2 tbsp olive oil
4 chicken breasts
8-12 small shallots
8 small garlic cloves
600ml (2½ cups) medium-dry white wine
2 tbsp fresh tarragon leaves, chopped, plus extra sprigs to garnish
4 fresh bay leaves
1 heaped tbsp crème fraîche

1. Heat a non-stick frying pan over a medium-high heat with one tablespoon of oil and add the chicken in one layer. Fry until golden on all sides. Set aside on a plate lined with kitchen paper.

2. Wipe the pan clean, return to the heat and add the remaining oil. Add the shallots and garlic and fry until lightly browned. Set aside with the chicken.

3. Add the wine to the pan and boil for 10 minutes, until reduced by three-quarters. Stir in 300ml (1¼ cups) of water, the tarragon and bay leaves. Return the chicken to the pan with the shallots and garlic. Cover and simmer for 20 minutes. Turn the chicken and cook, uncovered, for 25 minutes, until the sauce is reduced.

4. Lift the chicken into a serving bowl and scatter over the shallots and garlic. Stir the crème fraîche into the sauce, season with salt and pepper, pour over the chicken and serve with potatoes.

Per serving: *410kcals, 15.9g fat (4.8g saturated), 5.1g carbohydrates, 2.5g sugars, 38g protein, 0.6g fibre, 0.09g sodium*

LF DF GF

Easy lamb tagine

Serves 4

400g (14oz) lamb leg, cubed
2 tbsp olive oil
1 onion, sliced
2 garlic cloves, chopped
2 tsp ground coriander (cilantro)
2 tsp ground cumin
1 tsp ground ginger
Pinch ground cinnamon
1 cinnamon stick
1 x 400g (14oz) can chopped tomatoes
200ml (3/4 cup) chicken stock
100g (3.5oz) dried prunes or apricots
1 tbsp ground almonds
Handful of fresh coriander (cilantro), chopped

To serve:
Herbed couscous

1. Brown the lamb in the oil in a large pan and set aside. Add the onion and garlic and fry for five minutes.

2. Add the ground coriander, cumin, ginger and cinnamon and fry for two minutes.

3. Add the lamb, tomatoes and chicken stock. Add the prunes or apricots. Simmer for 40-45 minutes.

4. Stir in the ground almonds and fresh coriander. Serve with herbed couscous.

Per serving: *380kcals, 18.5g fat (4.7g saturated), 18.9g carbohydrates, 4.9g sugars, 35g protein, 0.5g fibre, 0.4g sodium*

LF DF

Lemon and olive chicken one pot

Serves 4

1kg (2.2lb) potatoes, such as Roosters
1 red (Spanish) onion, cut into wedges
75g (2.5oz) green olives
1 lemon, sliced
50g (2oz) streaky bacon, cut into strips
2 bay leaves
1 tbsp tomato purée
1 tbsp balsamic vinegar
120ml (½ cup) chicken stock
1 large chicken, jointed
1 tbsp olive oil
Salt and black pepper

1. Preheat the oven to 180˚C/160˚C fan/gas mark 4/350˚F.

2. Cut the potatoes into chunks and place in a roasting tin or ovenproof dish.

3. Squish in the onions, olives, lemon, bacon and bay leaves around the potatoes.

4. Stir the tomato purée and vinegar into the chicken stock and pour over the vegetables.

5. Lay the chicken on top, drizzle with olive oil and sprinkle with salt and pepper.

6. Roast for 50 minutes or until the chicken is golden brown. Transfer the chicken to a warm plate, cover and set aside to keep warm.

7. Increase the temperature to 220˚C/200˚C fan/gas mark 7/425˚F and return the dish to the oven for another 10 minutes. Place the chicken back on top of the vegetables and serve, family style!

Per serving: *358kcals, 9.9g fat (3.1g saturated), 52g carbohydrates, 1.57g sugars, 18g protein, 6g fibre, 0.9g sodium*

LF DF

Chicken paprika bake

Serves 4

600g (21oz) potatoes, peeled and chopped
1 tbsp paprika
2 tsp olive oil
2 onions, sliced
2 garlic cloves, crushed
2 red peppers (capsicums)
2 x 400g (14oz) cans chopped tomatoes
4 chicken breasts, cut in half

1. Preheat the oven to 200˚C/180˚C fan/gas mark 6/400˚F.

2. Add the potatoes to a large saucepan of water. Bring to the boil then simmer for 15-20 minutes until tender. Drain and mash.

3. Add one teaspoon of paprika to the mash and stir. Set aside.

4. Meanwhile, heat the oil in a large frying pan, add the onions and garlic and cook for a few minutes, until softened.

5. Stir in the paprika then add the peppers and tomatoes, let the mixture simmer.

6. Add in the chicken and continue to cook for five minutes.

7. Pour into a large ovenproof dish, spoon over the mash so that it covers the top and bake for 15 minutes until the mash is golden on top and the chicken cooked through.

Per serving: *402kcals, 11.2g fat (2.6g saturated), 42.8g carbohydrates, 11.2g sugars, 35.3g protein, 9.7g fibre, 0.11g sodium*

LF GF

Slow-cooker beef stew

Serves 8

2kg (4.4lb) stewing beef, cut into 2cm (1 inch) pieces
120g (1 cup) flour
70ml (4½ tbsp) olive oil
2 onions, chopped
170g (3/4 cup) tomato purée
240ml (1 cup) red wine
450g (16oz) potatoes, cut into 3cm (1.5 inch) pieces
200g (7oz) baby carrots
500ml (2 cups) beef broth/stock
1 tbsp salt
1 tsp dried thyme leaves
1 bay leaf
140g (1 cup) frozen peas, thawed

1. Coat the beef in the flour. Heat about half of the oil in a large frying pan over a medium-high heat. Brown the meat in batches then transfer to a slow cooker.

2. Add the onions to the pan and cook over a medium heat for 10 minutes until tender. Stir in the tomato purée and transfer to the slow cooker.

3. Pour the wine into the pan and scrape up any browned bits; add to the cooker. Stir in the potatoes, carrots, broth, salt, thyme and bay leaf.

4. Cover and cook on a low heat for seven hours, or on high for four hours. Add the peas and heat through.

Per serving: *714kcals, 24.5g fat (7.4g saturated), 32.3g carbohydrates, 6.8g sugars, 81.7g protein, 5.2g fibre, 1.3g sodium*

DF

Slow roasted Jamaican pork

Serves 4

3 tbsp olive oil
1kg (2.2lb) pork shoulder, cut into large chunks
2 onions, sliced
2 tbsp Jamaican jerk seasoning or paste
1 x 400g (14oz) can chopped tomatoes
1 garlic clove, crushed
1 red chilli, deseeded and finely sliced
300g (10.5oz) kale, shredded
Salt and black pepper

To serve:
Basmati rice, steamed

1. Heat the oven to 150°C/130°C fan/gas mark 2/300°F. Heat one tablespoon of the oil in a large saucepan over a medium-high heat. Add the pork and cook, stirring, for 4-5 minutes until browned on all sides. Transfer to a plate and set aside.

2. Add another tablespoon of oil and the onions and cook for 5-6 minutes until browned. Add the jerk seasoning or paste and cook for one minute.

3. Return the pork to the pan and stir in the tomatoes. Cover with a lid and cook in the oven for two hours until tender.

4. Heat the remaining oil in a frying pan over a medium-high heat. Add the garlic and chilli and cook for one minute until fragrant.

5. Stir in the kale and season with salt and pepper. Cook for 3-4 minutes until tender. Serve with the pork and basmati rice.

Per serving: *903kcals, 64.8g fat (21.3g saturated), 17.5g carbohydrates, 5g sugars, 62.4g protein, 3.8g fibre, 0.2g sodium*

DF

Lamb balti

Serves 4

2 tbsp olive oil
800g (28oz) lamb, trimmed and cut into chunks
1 brown onion, finely chopped
2 garlic cloves, crushed
3 tbsp balti curry paste
240ml (1 cup) beef stock
1 x 400g (14oz) can crushed tomatoes
100g (3.5oz) baby spinach

To serve:
Basmati rice

1. Heat one tablespoon of oil in a frying pan over a medium heat. Add the lamb in batches and cook for 3-5 minutes until browned. Transfer to a plate covered with kitchen paper.

2. Heat the remaining oil in a saucepan over a medium heat. Add the onion and garlic and cook for two minutes or until soft.

3. Add the curry paste, stirring, for three minutes. Gradually stir in the stock and tomatoes.

4. Return the lamb to the mixture along with any juices. Bring to the boil then reduce the heat to medium-low. Cover and simmer for one hour, stirring occasionally.

5. Remove the lid and simmer, stirring occasionally, for 30 minutes or until the lamb is tender and the sauce thickened slightly. Remove from the heat.

6. Stir in the spinach and cover for a minute until the spinach is just wilted. Serve the curry with rice.

Per serving: *558kcals, 29.3g fat (6.3g saturated), 11.4g carbohydrates, 3.9g sugars, 59.7g protein, 2.8g fibre, 0.3g sodium*

DF

Braised beef with noodles

Serves 4

2 tsp olive oil
1kg (2.2lb) beef stewing meat, cut into 3cm (1.5 inch) cubes
2 onions, sliced
2 garlic cloves, crushed
1 tbsp flour
240ml (1 cup) red wine
240ml (1 cup) beef stock
1 tbsp brown sugar
1 tbsp Worcestershire sauce
2 tbsp fresh rosemary leaves, chopped
200g (7oz) whole mushrooms
Salt and black pepper
1 bay leaf

To serve:
Curly egg noodles
A small handful of fresh parsley leaves, chopped

1. Heat the olive oil in a large saucepan over a medium-high heat. Add the beef and cook, turning, until it is browned on all sides.

2. Add the onion and cook for 7-8 minutes until softened. Stir in the garlic and cook for one minute.

3. Add the flour and cook for one minute, stirring constantly.

4. Stir in 420ml (1⅔ cup) of water and all the remaining ingredients. Cover, reduce the heat and simmer for one hour.

5. Uncover and simmer for 30 minutes until the beef is tender. Discard the bay leaf. Serve over the noodles and sprinkle with parsley.

Per serving: *632kcals, 15.5g fat (4.9g saturated), 14.9g carbohydrates, 6.6g sugars, 93.6g protein, 2.2g fibre, 0.39g sodium*

LF

One-pot sausage stew

Serves 4

4-6 sausages
1 tbsp olive oil
½ onion, finely chopped
2 garlic cloves, crushed
1 tsp ground cumin
1 tsp ground coriander (cilantro)
140g (¾ cup) long-grain rice
850ml (3½ cups) vegetable stock
1 x 400g (14oz) can chopped tomatoes
Salt and black pepper

1. Cut one end off of each sausage and cut down the centre of the sausage skins. Squeeze the meat out into a bowl. Using your hands, making sure they are clean, form small meatballs.

2. Heat the oil in a large, non-stick saucepan over a medium heat. Add the meatballs, in batches, and cook for a few minutes until browned on all sides. Transfer to a plate lined with kitchen paper.

3. Add the onion and garlic to the pan and cook for five minutes, stirring, until softened.

4. Add the cumin, coriander and rice and cook for another minute.

5. Pour in the stock and tomatoes and bring to a simmer. Cook for 10 minutes until the rice is just cooked.

6. Stir in the meatballs and season with salt and pepper. Cook for a few minutes until the meatballs are heated through. Ladle into bowls to serve.

Per serving: *830kcals, 37g fat (10.2g saturated), 73.1g carbohydrates, 6.1g sugars, 48.4g protein, 3.4g fibre, 1.3g sodium*

DF

Mighty and meatless

Aubergine Parmesan bake

Serves 6

2 garlic cloves, crushed
6 tbsp olive oil
2 x 400g (14oz) cans chopped tomatoes
2 tbsp tomato purée
4 aubergines (eggplants), cut into long, thin slices
75g (3/4 cup) Parmesan, grated
A handful of basil leaves, torn
1 egg, beaten

1. Heat oven to 200°C/180°C fan/gas mark 6/400°F. In a large, shallow saucepan, heat four tablespoons of the oil over a medium heat. Add the garlic and cook for three minutes.

2. Add the tomatoes, reduce the heat to low and simmer for eight minutes, stirring occasionally.

3. Stir in the tomato purée and continue to cook.

4. Heat a heavy frying pan or griddle pan over a high heat until very hot. Brush a few of the aubergine slices with a little oil and cook until well browned and cooked through, about three minutes per side. Transfer to a plate lined with kitchen paper and repeat with the remaining slices.

5. Line the bottom of an ovenproof baking dish with aubergine. Cover with the tomato sauce and sprinkle with Parmesan and basil leaves. Repeat until all the aubergine and sauce are used.

6. Pour the egg over the top of the bake, sprinkle with more Parmesan and bake in the oven for 20 minutes, or until the topping is golden.

Per serving: *460kcals, 28.9g fat (7.1g saturated), 41.2g carbohydrates, 18.8g sugars, 17.1g protein, 21.2g fibre, 0.36g sodium*

Healthy carrot and chickpea burgers

Serves 6

750g (26.5oz) carrots, peeled and grated
1 x 400g (14oz) can chickpeas, drained and rinsed
1 small onion, roughly chopped
2 tbsp tahini (sesame seed paste), plus 1 tsp to serve
1 tsp ground cumin
1 egg
3 tbsp olive oil
110g (1 cup) breadcrumbs
Zest of 1 lemon, plus 1 tsp juice
3 tbsp sesame seeds
140g (½ cup) natural yoghurt
6 burger buns

To serve:
Rocket (arugula) leaves
Red (Spanish) onion, sliced
Avocado, sliced
Chilli sauce

1. Put a third of the carrot in a food processor with the chickpeas, onion, two tablespoons of tahini, the cumin and egg. Pulse it until you have a thick paste. Transfer to a large bowl.

2. Heat one tablespoon of oil in a large, non-stick frying pan over a medium heat. Add the remaining carrot and cook for 8-10 minutes, stirring until the carrot is softened.

3. Add this cooked carrot to the paste with the breadcrumbs, lemon zest and sesame seeds. Season with salt and pepper and stir everything together.

4. Using your hands, making sure they are clean, form and shape the mixture into six burgers. Cover and chill until serving.

5. Mix the yoghurt with the remaining tahini and lemon juice then chill the mixture.

6. Heat a non-stick frying pan over a high heat and brush the burgers with the remaining oil. Cook the burgers for five minutes on each side, until golden and crisp.

7. Meanwhile, toast the burger buns. Serve each with some of the lemony sesame yoghurt, add the avocado, top with the burger, onion and rocket, or use toppings as to your liking. Finish with a drizzle of chilli sauce.

Per serving: *753 kcals, 31.6g fat (4.7g saturated), 96.5g carbohydrates, 19.5g sugars, 27g protein, 19.6g fibre, 0.4g sodium*

Low-fat vegetarian pie

Serves 4

1 tbsp vegetable oil
1 fennel bulb, chopped
½ onion, chopped
2 carrots, peeled and chopped
225g (3 cups) mushrooms, sliced
1 floury potato, peeled and chopped
Salt and black pepper
2 tbsp flour
240ml (1 cup) vegetable stock
240ml (1 cup) low-fat milk
145g (1 cup) frozen peas
A small handful of fresh chives, chopped
A small handful of fresh parsley leaves, chopped
1 tbsp white wine vinegar
1 sheet frozen puff pastry, thawed
1 egg yolk, beaten with 2 tsp of water

1. Preheat the oven to 200°C/180°C fan/gas mark 6/400°F. Heat the oil in a large saucepan over a medium heat and add the fennel, onion and carrots. Cook for three minutes until the onions are soft.

2. Add the mushrooms and potato and season with salt and pepper. Cook for five minutes until the mushrooms are browned.

3. Sprinkle over the flour, stirring to coat, and cook for one minute. Stir in the stock and milk until the mixture is smooth. Bring to a simmer and cook for five minutes until thickened.

4. Remove from the heat and stir in the peas, chives, parsley and vinegar. Pour the entire mixture into a baking dish.

5. Roll out the pastry dough on a lightly-floured surface and fit it to the top of the baking dish. Brush with the egg mixture and cut slits in the top of the pastry. Bake for 25-30 minutes until the pastry is puffed and golden.

Per serving: *281kcals, 9.7g fat (3.8g saturated), 40.4g carbohydrates, 9.7g sugars, 11.4g protein, 7.5g fibre, 0.26g sodium*

Mushroom pierogi with braised red cabbage

Serves 6

190g (1½ cups) flour
½ tsp salt
3 tbsp olive oil
80ml (⅓ cup) water
75g (1 cup) assorted mushrooms, finely chopped
1 small onion, finely chopped
Salt and black pepper
1 tbsp flour
25g (1oz) butter

For the cabbage:
1 medium red cabbage, quartered, cored and sliced
2 red (Spanish) onions, sliced
40g (⅓ cup) dried cranberries
2 apples, peeled, cored and grated
1 tsp ground cinnamon
2 tbsp demerara sugar
3 tbsp red wine vinegar
Salt and pepper

To serve:
Sour cream

1. Preheat the oven to 170°C/150°C fan/gas mark 3/325°F. For the cabbage, mix all of the ingredients together in a bowl and spoon into an ovenproof dish. Season well with salt and pepper and cover with tinfoil. Bake in the oven for 60-90 minutes until the cabbage is tender and juicy. Stir the ingredients 2-3 times during cooking.

2. To make the pierogi, add the flour, salt, oil and water in a large bowl and mix together until it forms a dough. Turn onto a lightly-floured surface and roll out thinly. Cut as many 12cm (5 inch) circles from the dough as possible.

3. Heat the oil in a saucepan over a medium high heat. Add the mushrooms and onions and cook until soft. Pour off any extra liquid that remains.

4. Stir the flour into the mushroom mixture.

5. Fill each dough circle with a small portion of the filling and fold in half. Gently seal the edge using a fork.

6. Bring a large pot of water with a pinch of salt to the boil over a high heat. Add the pierogi and cook for 5-7 minutes until they float.

7. Heat the butter in a saucepan over a medium heat. When the butter begins to foam, add the cooked pierogi and cook until they turn golden brown. Serve with braised cabbage and a dollop of sour cream.

Per serving: *333kcals, 10.8g fat (3.2g saturated), 54.7g carbohydrates, 18.2g sugars, 6.8g protein, 8.0g fibre, 0.25g sodium*

LF

Portobello stuffed potatoes

Serves 4

4 baked potatoes
2 tsp extra virgin olive oil
1 onion, sliced
2 Portobello mushrooms, stems removed and caps sliced
1 red pepper (capsicum), thinly sliced
2 tsp dried oregano
1 tbsp flour
60ml (¼ cup) vegetable stock
1 tbsp reduced-sodium soy sauce
100g (1 cup) Emmental cheese, sliced

1. Preheat the oven to 200˚C/180˚C fan/gas mark 6/400˚F and place the potatoes directly on the oven rack. Bake for 35-40 minutes until tender. Remove from the oven and slice down the centre of each potato. Use a fork to fluff up the insides.

2. Heat the oil in a large frying pan over a medium-high heat. Add the onion and cook for 2-3 minutes until it begins to soften. Add the mushrooms, pepper and oregano and cook for 5-7 minutes.

3. Reduce the heat and stir in the flour. Add the stock and soy sauce and bring to a simmer.

4. Remove from the heat and lay the Emmental over the top. Leave for 1-2 minutes until the cheese begins to melt.

5. Divide the mixture into four portions with a spatula, leaving the melted cheese layer on top. Scoop a portion into each potato and serve hot.

Per serving: *481kcals, 12.8g fat (5.5g saturated), 72.4g carbohydrates, 2.9g sugars, 20.1g protein, 7.6g fibre, 0.05g sodium*

DF

Roasted couscous-stuffed squash

Serves 4

260g (1½ cups) couscous
4 small squash, tops sliced off and centres scooped out
2 tbsp olive oil
30g (¼ cup) pistachios
A few sage leaves, chopped
2 tsp chilli pepper
4 tbsp dried cherries or cranberries

1. Soak the couscous in 250ml (1 cup) of water. Heat the oven to 200°C/180°C fan/gas mark 6/400°F and lightly coat the squash in oil. Roast the squash for 30-40 minutes or until tender.

2. Combine the remaining ingredients and use it to stuff the squash. Bake the squash with filling for a further 10 minutes.

Per serving: *417kcals, 14.6g fat (1.9g saturated), 60.2g carbohydrates, 3.4g sugars, 13.1g protein, 7g fibre, 0.02g sodium*

DF

Roasted vegetarian moussaka

Serves 4

2 aubergines (eggplants), sliced
2 courgettes (zucchinis), sliced
2 tbsp olive oil
1 large red pepper (capsicum), de-seeded and quartered
1 large yellow pepper (capsicum), de-seeded and quartered
Salt and black pepper
2 garlic cloves, peeled and finely chopped
180g (6 cups) spinach leaves
170ml (¾ cup) vegetable stock
1 x 400g (14oz) can chopped tomatoes, drained
2 x 400g (14oz) cans cannellini beans
2 tbsp tomato purée
1 tsp ground cinnamon
4 slices of Halloumi

1. Preheat the oven to 200˚C/180˚C fan/gas mark 6/400˚F. Toss the aubergines, courgettes and peppers with 1½ tablespoons of oil, salt and pepper and arrange in a single layer on a baking tray. Cook for 20 minutes, or until tender.

2. Meanwhile, heat the remaining oil in a frying pan over a medium heat and stir in half of the garlic. Cook for one minute, then add the spinach and cook until it wilts.

3. In a saucepan over a low heat, combine the stock, tomatoes, beans, purée and cinnamon and cook, stirring occasionally, for 15 minutes until the mixture becomes thick.

4. Once the vegetables are cooked, place a slice of halloumi over four aubergines and grill for two minutes or until the cheese melts.

5. Alternate the vegetables with the bean mixture and top with a Halloumi-covered aubergine slice.

6. Season with pepper and serve hot.

Per serving: *936kcals, 13.8g fat (3.9g saturated), 156g carbohydrates, 1.9g sugars, 8.0g protein, 66.2g fibre, 0.16g sodium*

LF DF

Vegetable lentil curry

Serves 4

2 tsp olive oil
1 red (Spanish) onion, cut into wedges
1 garlic clove, crushed
2 tbsp mild curry paste
1 red pepper (capsicum), sliced
1 head of cauliflower, cut into small florets
110g (1½ cups) mushrooms, quartered
1 aubergine (eggplant), sliced
1 x 400g (14oz) can chopped tomatoes
240ml (1 cup) vegetable stock
300g (2 cups) green beans, trimmed
1 x 400g (14oz) can brown lentils, drained and rinsed
A handful of fresh coriander (cilantro) leaves, chopped

To serve:
Natural yoghurt
Boiled rice

1. Heat the oil in a saucepan over a medium-high heat. Add the onion and garlic and cook for 2-3 minutes until soft.

2. Add the curry paste and cook for one minute or until it becomes fragrant.

3. Add the red pepper, cauliflower, mushroom, aubergine, tomato and stock and bring to the boil. Reduce the heat and simmer, covered, for 10-12 minutes until the vegetables are tender.

4. Add the green beans and lentils and cook for three minutes until the beans are tender and lentils heated through. Serve with rice and natural yoghurt.

Per serving: *464kcals, 6.9g fat (0g saturated fat), 74.3g carbohydrates, 10.9g sugars, 28.6g protein, 19.1g fibre, 0.2g sodium*

LF

Vegetarian chilli

Serves 6-8

2 x 400g (14oz) cans chopped tomatoes
950ml (4 cups) vegetable stock
1 x 400g (14oz) can black beans
1 x 400g (14oz) can cannellini beans
1 x 400g (14oz) can kidney beans
1 onion, chopped
1 green pepper (capsicum), chopped
2 garlic cloves, crushed
2 jalapeño peppers, chopped
1 tsp dried oregano
1 tsp ground cumin
2-3 dashes of Tabasco sauce
85g (½ cup) quinoa
115g (1 cup) Cheddar, grated
A handful of fresh coriander (cilantro) leaves, chopped

1. Combine all the ingredients except for the quinoa, Cheddar and coriander in a large saucepan over a medium-low heat. Cover and cook for two hours.

2. Ten minutes before serving, uncover and stir in the quinoa. Cook until tender.

3. Spoon into serving bowls and top with Cheddar and fresh coriander leaves.

Per serving: *610kcals, 3.8g fat (1g saturated), 107.7g carbohydrates, 7.8g sugars, 40.4g protein, 31g fibre, 0.16g sodium*

LF DF

Veggie tagine

Serves 4

4 carrots, peeled and diced
4 small parsnips, peeled and diced
3 red (Spanish) onions, peeled and cut into wedges
2 red peppers (capsicum), deseeded and diced
2 tbsp olive oil
1 tsp ground cumin
1 tsp paprika
1 tsp cinnamon
1 tsp mild chilli powder
1 x 400g (14oz) can chopped tomatoes
2 tbsp soft dried apricots
2 tsp honey

To serve:
Couscous

1. Heat the oven to 200°C/180°C fan/gas mark 6/400°F. Scatter the vegetables onto a couple of baking trays, drizzle with half the oil, season, then toss with your hands to coat. Roast in the oven for 30 minutes until tender and beginning to brown.

2. Meanwhile, place a large frying pan over a medium heat. Add the remaining oil, ground cumin, paprika, cinnamon and chilli powder and heat for one minute until they release their fragrance.

3. Add the tomatoes, fill the empty can with water and add to the mixture, plus the apricots and honey. Simmer for five minutes until the sauce is slightly reduced and the apricots have rehydrated.

4. Stir in the roast vegetables and season with salt and pepper. Cook for one minute. Serve with couscous.

Per serving: *263kcals, 8.2g fat (1.2g saturated), 47.8g carbohydrates, 20g sugars, 4.7g protein, 11.8g fibre, 0.07g sodium*

Recipe index

Budget-Friendly · Freezable · Kid-Friendly · Low-Fat · Diabetes-Friendly · Gluten-Free